A COLORSLIDE

Cleveland of Art

SHERMAN E. LEE

32 MASTERPIECES

TOUR OF THE

Museum

CLEVELAND, OHIO

INTING VISITED WITH

SHERMAN E. LEE, DIRECTOR

On the end papers:
Special Exhibition Gallery, New Wing

THIS BOOK HAS BEEN PREPARED UNDER THE
SUPERVISION OF HARRY N. ABRAMS, INC.

COLORSLIDE INDEX

Your guide for this Colorslide Tour

is **SHERMAN E. LEE**

Director of the Cleveland Museum of Art

Dr. Lee is one of the youngest directors of a major American museum, and although it was only in April, 1958, that he was appointed to his present position, he has already distinguished himself with brilliant purchases, striking exhibitions, and imaginative museum administration. His career is rather unusual in that he received his early art training in the Museum he now directs. He received his Ph.D. at Western Reserve University, in Cleveland, in 1941, and in the same year became Curator of Far Eastern Art at the Detroit Institute of Art. In 1948 he was appointed Assistant Director, and, later, Associate Director of the Seattle Art Museum. He returned to Cleveland to become Curator of Oriental Art in 1952, and in 1957 he became Associate Director of the Museum. Along with his other duties, he shared supervision of an extensive program of construction and adaptation which greatly enlarged the Museum, making it one of the most exciting institutions of its kind in the world. In addition to his curatorial and scholarly activities, Dr. Lee is dedicated to the continuance of the public services for which this Museum has become renowned.

THE STORY OF THE
Cleveland Museum of Art

To supplement the paintings visited on the tour, these introductory pages show important works of art from other departments in the great collections of the Museum.

TO REACH the Cleveland Museum of Art from the center of the city, you drive east out Euclid Avenue, passing the sites of the now almost vanished mansions of Cleveland's "first families." You come to University Circle after leaving the commercial section, and enter a unique cultural area—with the Museum, the symphony orchestra's Severance Hall, Western Reserve University, Case Institute of Technology, and many other institutions close together. On the far side of a small lake which is surrounded by a lovely Fine Arts Garden, stands the Art Museum. Your first glance at it reveals a moderate-sized, Neo-Classic marble structure facing south, rather simpler and more subtle than most. As you drive around the east side of the building toward the rear, you arrive at the parking lot by the North Entrance, and now the new addition to the Museum comes into view—a modern gray and rose granite structure, well integrated with the older building but connected to it by glass window-walled galleries. The old and the new seem not incongruous enemies but individuals of different characters accustomed to friendly accommodation to each other's idiosyncrasies. Old and new, individuals, different characters, and accommodation—these have made the whole fabric of the institution, whether real or intangible.

As American cities go, Cleveland has a respectable age, having been founded in 1794 by settlers from

A MOURNER
*by Claus de Werve
French, active 1398-1439
J. H. Wade Collection*

New England. But it was not until 1916 that a real art museum was opened to the public. The will had been there earlier, for in 1882 Jeptha Homer Wade gave Wade Park to the city with the understanding that a cultural center would be placed there. At about the same time, unknown to each other, John Huntington, Horace Kelley, and Hinman B. Hurlbut had left money for an art museum. The legal ingenuity and tenacious good will of succeeding public-minded Trustees made it possible for these four bequests to be combined in 1913, and the simple, balanced, but flexible Neo-Classic building was the result.

The founding and growth of the Museum are evidence of the finest aspirations of public-spirited and art-loving individuals, of whom Cleveland has had so many. All of the Museum's money comes from funds given or bequeathed by private sources and from individual memberships. No money is received from municipal, state, or national sources; yet the Museum is open free to the public and provides one of the oldest and broadest educational programs of any such institution in the United States.

RELIEF FROM THE PALACE
OF ASHURNASIRPAL II
Assyrian
9th century B.C.
J. H. Wade Collection

CHRIST AND ST. JOHN
German
about 1280
J. H. Wade Collection

The growth of the Museum has been phenomenal. Beginning with a good but scattered collection—including the second collection of Italian painting formed by the pioneer collector James Jackson Jarves, acquired by Liberty E. Holden in 1884 and given to the Museum—it has added great works of art in all fields. Like the Metropolitan Museum or the Louvre, it is not just a picture gallery, but exhibits all of the arts, as its departmental names indicate: Paintings; Prints and Drawings; Decorative Arts; Egyptian and Classical Art; Near Eastern Art; Oriental Art; Textiles. The great trust funds owned by or contributing to the Museum have made the growth possible and bear some of the most prominent names of the city's history: Dudley P. Allen; Leonard C. Hanna, Jr.; Delia E. and Liberty E. Holden; Mr. and Mrs. William H. Marlatt; Elisabeth S. Prentiss; Grace Rainey Rogers; John L. Severance; J. H. Wade; and numerous others.

The Medieval Collection, with its great 11th- and 12th-century gold objects from the famous Guelph Treasure, has long been the cornerstone of the Museum's international reputation, and it is certainly true that any serious student of Medieval German art must pay a visit to Cleveland. But the Thirties and then the Forties saw much growth in other areas: Pre-Columbian Art of the Americas, American Painting, Old Masters, and Far Eastern Art, among others, gave the Museum a balanced collection of fine works of art in every field. Throughout this period of growth, the Museum applied only the highest standards in acquiring works of art. This policy has determined the character of the Museum's collections—not as large as some, but of uniformly high quality. The old building became more and more crowded and the need for an addition more apparent. Using monies from nearly all the sources named above, the largest share coming from Hanna Fund and The John Huntington Art and Polytechnic Trust, and from individual contributions, the new wing was completed and opened in March, 1958. The old building had been refurbished as well, and now the visitor is treated to a succession of galleries, varied in size, height, color, lighting, and manner of presentation. The fairest compliments about the galleries are not that they are imposing or grand, but that they are continuously stimulating, human in scale, and do not induce the "museum-fatigue" so prevalent in the marble palaces of, or inspired by, the past.

An art museum is first a storehouse where works of art *worth preserving* are kept and shown. The American museum has added a second function now more and more admired abroad—education. And, since it is an *art* museum—not one of history, science, or technology—art must be its first concern for preservation, exhibition, and education. The temporary exhibitions in the new and flexible special exhibition gallery, the adult and children's classes in gallery or classroom, and publications like our *Bulletin* and catalogues should all help us to see what the great artists and craftsmen have tried

TAPESTRY PANEL
Late Hellenistic
3rd-5th century A.D.
J. H. Wade Collection

GERTRUDIS PORTABLE ALTAR
German, Lower Saxony
about 1040
John Huntington Collection

STREAMS AND
MOUNTAINS WITHOUT END
Chinese
Northern Sung dynasty
early 12th *century*
Gift of Hanna Fund

NATARAJA: LORD OF THE DANCE
South Indian
Chola period, 11th century
J. H. Wade Collection

to make us see in their chosen medium in the visual arts. Romance, names, history, and technique may or may not be helpful, but without the original work we cannot really know art. In Cleveland, the art and art history students learn their lessons on technique, composition, stylistic analysis, or the art of the Renaissance and other periods directly from great, original works of art. The pills which the textbooks offer are balanced by immediate experience, and many a theory which can fly in the austere atmosphere of the classroom comes to grief against the true face of art. Thus one learns not just a roll call of "great" names in art, but how to compare, evaluate, and finally to *see*.

Let us begin, then, on our brief tour. We stand in the Rotunda of the old building facing Gallery One, the gallery of Early Medieval Art. The Rotunda has something in it of the measured space of the Classical world and also something of the dim light of the decline and fall of Rome. Here, amid Early Christian objects, we will step forward on the first stage of the artistic journey of Western man.

AND NOW YOUR
COLORSLIDE TOUR BEGINS—

SLIDE 1

We start our tour with illuminated manuscripts—so called because they glow with precious gold and vivid colors. Before printing was invented, books were lettered and decorated by hand, and this became a major form of painting. Here is a page of an illuminated manuscript from the Byzantine Empire—a continuation of the Roman Empire in eastern Europe—whose capital at Constantinople was, until the twelfth century, the sophisticated, urban center of the Christian world where East met West. We see St. Luke, dressed in a Roman toga, and seated in a Classical arched niche, gazing rigidly at us. His draperies are arranged in a geometric linear pattern, and his head and shoulders are sharply silhouetted against the gold background. The general composition and the technique of modeling in light and shade are still indebted to the art of Classical Rome, but the rich, jewel-like color is Oriental, and the severe, religious intensity is peculiarly Byzantine. Manuscripts were easily carried from place to place, enabling artists all over Europe to absorb influences from distant sources. Byzantine manuscripts were one of the starting points for the new style called "Romanesque," which developed in Western Europe after 1000 A.D.

1. Page from a Manuscript: St. Luke

BYZANTINE, MIDDLE ELEVENTH CENTURY

J. H. Wade Collection

2. Page from a
Manuscript: St. Matthew

GERMAN, SAXON, END TWELFTH CENTURY

J. H. Wade Collection

SLIDE 2

Here is a manuscript illumination, exhibited around the corner from the Byzantine page we just saw, and almost as close in time. It is a German Romanesque page, made by an unknown co-worker of Hermann of Helmarshausen (HELL-*mars-hows-en*), under the patronage of Henry the Lion, who returned from the Crusades in 1175. This one represents St. Matthew, and uses the same color and gold technique as the Byzantine page. But what an enormous difference otherwise! Where the Eastern page is a simple composition with broad areas, this one is complex, with a great use of a curling, interlaced decoration that recalls the pre-Christian geometric ornamental art of the nomadic European tribes—"Wandering Folk." We feel an almost barbaric vigor in the bold and uninhibited profusion of movement and countermovement. The differences between the two pages, between Classical balanced space and European vigorous complexity, can be seen again in later European painting in the opposition of North and South Europe—slides eight and nine, for example. The interaction between the two regions and styles was a healthy one for the development of painting.

Moving now into the painting galleries, we enter what is called the "primitive" age of European painting. Nineteenth-century critics saw little mastery in such altar panels as this well-preserved example by Lippo Memmi of Siena. The gold background, the formal poses, and the unearthly seriousness of the faces reminded them of Byzantine art and seemed a far cry from the masterworks of Raphael (RAF-*ay-ell*) and Michelangelo (*mickel*-AHN-*jell-oh*). But we now see the formal Byzantine style as a major source for early Italian painting; and we are also aware of a new feeling in the exquisite tenderness and subtle modeling of hands and faces. The Child's appealing and natural gesture of the right hand would have been quite foreign to the earlier, Byzantine masters. This delight in the observed world is delicately balanced with a still dominant religious mood, so characteristic of the time of St. Francis; and it led to new heights of art, with the names of Cimabue (*chee-mah*-BOO-*eh*), Giotto (JAWT-*toh*), and Duccio (DOOT-*choh*) on the summits. The medieval tradition of fine craftsmanship is evident in the splendid tooling of the gold.

3. *Madonna and Child*

by LIPPO MEMMI

(Sienese, active 1317-1347)

Gift of Hanna Fund

The fourteenth-century Sienese style of the last picture was exported to France during the period of Papal residence at Avignon (*ah-vee*-NYON). It spread over France, England, Germany, and Austria, and has been called the "International Gothic" style. We are now fairly certain that this little *Annunciation* was painted in the region of Paris, about 1390. Its tooled back imitates bookbinding, and therefore recalls delicate manuscripts. The gold background is thoroughly medieval, but there is a modern spirit in the Virgin's throne, which is successful in providing a limited stage that places her in space. The reading stand establishes the point nearest the spectator; and the angel's scroll and left hand not only relate the figures to each other but connect the nearer things in space with the farther. The artist is as much concerned with these new spatial problems as with color, precision of outline, and pattern. Indeed, at the top of the picture, the old and new are side by side: note the abstract circles enclosing God the Father, and the carefully constructed canopy with its realistic, parallel perspective.

This picture was separated from the Parisian Gothic *Annunciation* by only ten years of time but over five hundred miles of distance. It was painted in the monastery of Heiligenkreuz (HIGH-*lih-gen-kroytz*)—which means Holy Cross—by an artist in Austria whose name we do not know but whom we call the Master of Heiligenkreuz, after the place where he worked. This *Death of the Virgin* belongs to the International Gothic style, but the figures are more crowded and agitated than in French and Italian paintings. Most of the figures are forced into the background, where they demonstrate sorrow by angular movements of their exaggeratedly thin, long arms or by the expressions of their almost Byzantine faces. But the new spirit can be seen in the intense concentration of the reading Evangelist at the lower left, who is keenly observed even to the careful depiction of the spectacles—one of the earliest representations of this attribute of the bookworm. Nevertheless, the *Death of the Virgin* is a conservative work for its time, and the rich color, reaching its gayest peak in St. Peter's Christmas-tree-like headdress, seems close to manuscript illumination.

4. *Annunciation*

FRENCH, SCHOOL OF PARIS, ABOUT 1390

Mr. and Mrs. William H. Marlatt Collection

5. *The Death of the Virgin*

by the MASTER OF HEILIGENKREUZ (Austrian, early fifteenth century)

Gift of Friends of the Museum

One of the most unusual panels in the gallery of early northern European painting is *The Two Lovers,* probably done near Ulm, Germany. This painting does not remind us of the religious pictures we have just studied but, rather, of secular, everyday art, particularly tapestries, with their foliage-patterned backgrounds and subjects derived from ideals of chivalric love. The gay colors and elegant proportions of the figures recall the moods evoked by the troubadors and minnesingers, and their songs of courtly romance. However, as in most medieval works, religion and morality are also present in what appears to be nonreligious subject matter. Furthermore, on the reverse side of this panel there once was a chilling representation of two skeletons in poses similar to those of the two lovers. The *memento mori*—reminder of death— was common in Gothic and even later times. To this we all come—and yet the artist bestowed the better part of his time and talent on the betrothed couple. Numerous engravings by such great early German masters as Schongauer (SHONE-*gow-er*), the so-called Master E. S., and others demonstrate the popularity of similar subjects of courtly dalliance.

6. *The Two Lovers*

GERMAN, SWABIAN SCHOOL, ABOUT 1470

Holden Collection

7. *The Nativity*

by GERARD DAVID

(Flemish, about 1450-1523)

Purchased from the Leonard C. Hanna, Jr., Bequest

Gerard David (DAH-*vitt*) was, with Memling, the last great follower of the richly colored, atmospheric, and highly realistic style established in Flanders early in the fifteenth century by the brothers Hubert and Jan van Eyck (*van* IKE) and Rogier van der Weyden (*roh*-JEER *van dare* VYE-*denn*). The glowing unity of color in this *Nativity* is due to the new technique of painting in oil perfected by Jan van Eyck. As far and as closely as one looks, details are microscopically true, as if the painter sought to fix reality forever on the wooden panel. The flowered foreground still recalls secular tapestries and miniatures of the International Gothic style, but the landscape as a whole is not unlike those in larger Gothic miniature paintings, where the first real landscapes appeared. The Flemish conquest of atmospheric space unifies foreground and background, and points the way to the spacious landscapes of Bruegel (BREW-*gell*). We see the influence of the "new" Renaissance manner in the spacing of the almost monumental figures, particularly in the dominant figure of Joseph, obviously a portrait—another sign of the diminishing religious fervor and the growing interest in man as an ordinary human being.

8. *The Stag Hunt*

by LUCAS CRANACH (German, 1472-1553)

John L. Severance Collection

Although later by some fifty years than *The Nativity*, Lucas Cranach's (KRAH-*nock's*) *Stag Hunt*, like most German painting of the early sixteenth century, seems more conservative in style. The leafy forest recalls the *Two Lovers* and Gothic tapestries; and the tightly enclosed composition echoes the desire of the hunters to round up the stags. The subject of the picture is completely nonreligious; with its portraits of the Grand Duke John Frederick the Magnanimous of Saxony and his numerous family, as well as a background "portrait" of the hunting castle, *Hartenfels* (Stag Rock), it commemorates an actual hunt. The hunt had long been a popular subject, but to make a souvenir, a picture of a given hunt, was a modern note in art at this time. Pictures like this are meant to be "read" part by part, and much of their appeal depends upon wealth of narrative detail. Although the main participants are the noble hunters and their even nobler prey, the outer reaches of the painting show more lowly types attacking and being attacked by bears, while lesser animals scurry for cover.

We retrace our steps to Gallery Three, where we stop before an arched panel of the Italian Renaissance, by Baldovinetti (*bal-doh-vih-*NATE-*tee*) or his school—and now look upon a new and different world. The mood of this painting is relaxed, and one of the mottoes of Classical antiquity is suggested: measure in all things. Everything is measured and formal—the verticals of the tree trunks, the stately recession of the distant pines, the deep, sculptural folds of the adoring Madonna. But there is also a lively interest in nature, whether in the nude Christ Child—so different from the tiny, almost doll-like baby of the Gerard David *Nativity*—or in the representation of the valley of the Arno near Florence. Medieval symbolism remains in the left middle distance, where the young Tobias, carrying the fish and guided by the angel, prefigures Christ and His Passion. The colors of this picture are subdued and somewhat dry, partly because it was done with tempera paint—that is, color mixed in an egg-and-water emulsion—and partly because the artist thought of objects as tinted sculpture, modeled in light and shade, rather than as the surfaces of glowing color that we have seen in Northern painting.

9. *Madonna and Child*

SCHOOL OF BALDOVINETTI
(Florentine, fifteenth century)

Holden Collection

This is one of the finest works by Filippino Lippi, son of Fra Filippo Lippi and pupil of Botticelli (*bot-tih*-CHEL-*lee*). Here we see a highly conscious art, typical of the last quarter of the fifteenth century when Leonardo, Michelangelo, and Raphael were about to create a new "High" Renaissance style, simpler and more massive and full-bodied than the linear and decorative mode of Botticelli's circle. The linear and undulating rhythms, the pale and aristocratic faces, and such Classical details as the column with its capital, are a heritage from Botticelli, but are here somewhat "mannered," or exaggerated. The circular *tondo*, a peculiarly Renaissance and Florentine shape not used by the northern European painters, had a strong appeal to the intellectually minded painters, who were very much at home in geometry and philosophy. To compose figures within a circle and achieve a stable result was a most difficult problem solved in only a few famous examples, including this. Without the column and, at right angles to it, the ledge and cross of St. John with the basket pinning down the point of intersection, the composition would roll away to oblivion.

10. *The Holy Family with Margaret and St. John*

by FILIPPINO LIPPI (Florentine, about 1457-1504)

Holden Collection

11. *Sacrifice of Abraham*

by ANDREA DEL SARTO (Florentine, 1486-1531)

Holden Collection

The heroic scale of these figures—their grand and dramatic poses, if nothing else—would signify the change that occurred in Italian art about 1500. Before, one could see a Renaissance picture part by part and add all up to a whole; now, in a new unity, all parts were fused into one impression of grandeur and amplitude. Drawing the human figure had by now become second nature to the artist and he could reach for more elaborate and dramatic gestures and poses. Andrea del Sarto was one of the greatest draftsmen—a rival of Michelangelo—and his mastery is demonstrated in this unfinished panel, with its preliminary drawing still visible under the thin paint. The artists of the sixteenth century also began to play boldly with effects of space and distance. Here the sudden thrust of Abraham's right arm, the diagonal placement of the altar, and the foreshortening of the angel's muscular little body are a means of opening up the space cleverly suggested in the picture. Vasari, who wrote his *Lives of the Most Eminent Painters* in 1550, said of this composition, "... he is judged never at any time to have accomplished a work of more perfect excellence."

The Venetian painters of the High Renaissance developed a totally new approach to painting. The Florentines first made a careful drawing and modeled the shadowed areas before they gave a painting its color. But the Venetians *painted directly* in color with much less attention to outline or detail. Their art was more visual, with things painted as they are *seen* rather than as they are *known*. Oil painting, which had been used by the Flemish masters for both atmosphere and detail, became in Venice a flexible medium for hazy distances, tremulous contours, and modeling by color alone. In this respect the Venetians were the ancestors of the nineteenth-century Impressionist painters. In his own career, Titian (TISH-*un*) passed through all the stages of sixteenth-century development to this *Adoration of the Magi*. It was painted about 1560 for Philip II of Spain, whose likeness is used for the first adoring king. The easy flow of the composition and the ample gestures of the figures are characteristic of the relaxed and sensuous Venetian tradition. The silvery color provides a cool and tranquil setting for the joyous event. Popes, kings, and high officials competed for Titian's services. In return, the shrewd Venetian received honors, titles, and pensions.

12. Adoration of the Magi

by TITIAN (Venetian, 1477-1576)

Mr. and Mrs. William H. Marlatt Collection

13. Baptism of Christ

by TINTORETTO (Venetian, 1518-1594)

Gift of Hanna Fund

SLIDE 13

This *Baptism* hangs in the Museum's spacious Armor Court, where its large dimensions can breathe more easily. Tintoretto (*tin-toh-*RET-*toh*) was a Venetian, like Titian, and, in his own way, as great a painter. He cared little for money or honors, and sought only to release his gigantic energy in work. In his own words, his art attempted to combine "the color of Titian and the drawing of Michelangelo." His large canvases are intensely dramatic, and teem with elongated but muscular and richly painted figures. They have been aptly compared, in their opulence and variety, to Shakespeare's plays, with their plots and counterplots, their frenzied activity and ominous calm. John, in the act of baptizing, is daringly foreshortened, his energy contrasted with the passiveness of Christ, who seems the center of an almost circular composition set into the rectangle of the frame. The distant landscape, the ocean, and the burst of heavenly light about the Holy Ghost are painted very freely; on close examination, all detail is lost, yet at a distance the vigorous brush strokes seem to fuse to produce a lively effect. The allegorical figure of the river god at the right, derived from Classical antiquity, is painted in a brusque style, emphasizing the planes of the muscles, that points the way to the Post-Impressionism of Cézanne (*say-*ZAHN), which we shall see later.

14. *The Holy Family*

by EL GRECO (Spanish, 1541-1614)

Gift of Friends of the Museum

We move now to Gallery Six, where the soft, warm, brown linen walls provide a rich setting for the sumptuous Baroque art of the seventeenth century. The word "Baroque"—meaning uneven, irregular—is a term at first used disparagingly to refer to the style of the time of the Counter Reformation. Tintoretto was probably the teacher of El Greco, who originally came from the island of Crete and later moved to Toledo, in Spain. El Greco, one of the great geniuses of art, was ignored for more than two centuries. Around the beginning of our own century, his violent distortions and extreme emotionalism found a ready audience, though for aesthetic rather than the original religious reasons, and his greatness was recognized. El Greco's theatrical tendencies, embodied in his twisting figures with their intense faces and liquid eyes, are Baroque. However, his tightly knit compositions, with their rather metallic-looking draperies forced toward the spectator, are half way between High Renaissance and Baroque, showing the characteristics of a period and style called "Mannerism." In this *Holy Family*, sky and draperies seem one, joined by a flickering light on edges and crests, in a nervous, restless movement. Nearly all of the hands frame a brilliant still life of cherries in a glass bowl.

Murillo (*moo*-REE-*lyoh*) is the most characteristic Spanish Baroque artist. One of his great contemporaries, Velázquez (*veh*-LATH-*keth*), was chiefly a painter of secular subjects, and another, Zurbarán (*thoor-bah*-RAHN), was too austere to be fully representative of the style. Murillo has often been accused of sentimentality, and, to be sure, there is sentiment here in the upturned eyes of the Virgin, as well as in the gently smiling angels; but the airy, transparent color, the sure drawing, and the marvelous suggestion of figures floating keep the emotion controlled. Murillo is famous for his paintings of the Immaculate Conception of the Virgin, one of the most important church doctrines during the Counter Reformation. The subject was repeated often in workshop canvases or even cruder copies. It became stiff and sentimental, subtracting much luster in modern times from Murillo's fame, which was very high in the eighteenth and nineteenth centuries. He was a true innovator in color, for the pale, cool tonalities anticipate the color schemes of the eighteenth century, and his cherubic angels provided the models for the delightful creations of the later French masters, Boucher (*boo*-SHAY) and Fragonard (*frah-gaw*-NAHR).

15. The Immaculate Conception

by MURILLO (Spanish, 1617-1682)

Purchased from the

Leonard C. Hanna, Jr., Bequest

The upper part of this picture by Poussin (*poo*-SAN), with its billowing clouds and angels in pale colors, is not unlike the painting by Murillo that we just saw. But the scene below shows a different side of the seventeenth century—cool, rational, and influenced by the period's concept of Classical antiquity. Poussin, although French, lived mostly in Rome, where his keen, logical mind created its own blend of solid Classical form and rich Venetian color. St. Joseph and the oarsman could easily be Roman nobles, and the Christ Child a young Dionysus (*dye-oh*-NY-*sus*). The tranquil landscape echoes the calm and measured movements of the larger figures. The adult figures are unaware of the Christ Child's vision of his future crucifixion. Across the water, Jonah stands beneath grapevines. He is a symbol of passage from the Old Testament to the New—of rebirth, and of the Resurrection. In the middle distance is a crowned figure holding a harp, probably King David, the ancestor of Christ. The frowning and forbidding boatman may be meant as Charon (KAY-*ron*), the awesome mythological figure who ferried the dead across the River Styx into Hades. Poussin had good precedent for such combinations in Dante's *Divine Comedy*.

16. Flight Into Egypt

by POUSSIN (French, 1594-1665)

Gift of Hanna Fund

17. *Portrait of Charles II, King of England*

by PHILIPPE DE CHAMPAIGNE (French, 1602-1674)

Elisabeth Severance Prentiss Collection

While Poussin worked in Rome, others flourished amid the intrigues and formalities of the dazzling court of Louis XIV, the Sun King. Portraits were in demand, but flattery often reduced them to the level of aristocratic pot-boilers. Perhaps the finest French portraitist of the seventeenth century was Philippe de Champaigne (*fil*-LEEP *duh sham*-PAIN-*yeh*), who was of Flemish origin. The severity of his best work contrasts with the pomposity of the court painters. This portrait of the future Charles II of England was painted in 1653, in France, at Saint Germain, where the prince and his mother took refuge from Cromwell's Commonwealth. Charles—"Old Rowley," as he was later called—gazes at the painter with a cold disdainful eye, but the artist does not flinch. The prince's strength and guile are frankly revealed, and the prophecy—which came true—is made that he will return to England as a victor, for his baton points to an invasion fleet and the cliffs of Dover across the English Channel. The cold blue ribbon and the silvery haze of the sea-scape provide a telling counterpoint to the warm black of the armor and the red sash. Champaigne's mastery is seen in the beautifully drawn and firmly painted hands.

18. Diana and Her Nymphs Departing for the Chase

by RUBENS (Flemish, 1577-1640)   *Purchased from the Leonard C. Hanna, Jr., Bequest*

19. A Genoese Lady with Her Child

by VAN DYCK (Flemish, 1599-1641)

Gift of Hanna Fund

Rubens, the "Prince of Painters," was a completely successful artist—fortunate in love, skillful in diplomacy, and a towering figure among northern Baroque masters. His subject matter was varied—Catholic or pagan, landscape or portraiture; and most of his works have an easy grandeur and a flowing, masterful technique. The large mythological pictures are paeans to sensuous delight. Diana, the chaste goddess, stands proud and serene amid earthier companions—three nymphs and two satyrs. The blond tonality of the picture is the result of thin and well-controlled films of color over a solid underpainting. Rubens' pictures are usually well preserved. There is an infinite number of themes and variations—the play of feet and hands, the vistas to a low-lying landscape, the varied textures, the different kinds of skin, from the virile tan of the amorous satyr to the pearly glow of Diana's skin, and especially the weaving in-and-out movement of the figures in space. Not one limb or hand is uncertain of its place in the composition; the drawing of the foreshortened arms is breath-takingly simple and accurate. This large canvas, painted about 1620, is one of the artist's finest pagan subjects painted at the height of his first original and creative period.

Van Dyck's (*van* DIKE'*s*) short career included a four-year stay in Italy, where he painted numerous full-length portraits which are among his finest works. In portraiture, he was the first to exploit systematically the viewpoint from below, in order to add aristocratic dignity and physical height to his sitters. In contrast to Philippe de Champaigne, who *observed* Charles II, Van Dyck *admired* this noble lady and her charming daughter. The figures, though freely painted, are carefully finished; but the background with its drape and column are sketchily and hazily shown, thus allowing the eye to focus on the relation of mother and child. The stiffness of red brocade adds further dignity to the lady; and the black lace ruff and wristlets are final touches of distinction. The blue velvet adds a harmonious note of softness to the child. Even the hands are a consistent part of the relation, the mother's firm and long, the girl's curling and soft. Van Dyck later took this polished style to England and there founded the important English portrait school.

20. *Portrait of a Lady Standing*

by TERBORCH (Dutch, 1617-1681)

Elisabeth Severance Prentiss Collection

SLIDE 20

Rubens and Van Dyck were products of the Flemish Baroque, with its Catholic and aristocratic background. Holland was fully independent after the Peace of Westphalia in 1648 and, although next to Flanders geographically, produced an utterly different art out of a Protestant, middle-class background. Terborch's (*ter*-BORK's) lady is as well dressed as Van Dyck's, and may well have been wealthier; but she is shown in small scale, related to table and chair rather than drape and column. The exquisite finish of the details is quite different from the broader, Venetian manner of the Flemish masters. In his small, quiet world, Terborch specialized in certain textures. No one, before him or since, has been able to render the velvets, satins, laces, and brocades of Dutch ladies with such sensitivity and skill. The suggested space is ordered by a subtle play of light of a kind brought to an even higher pitch by Vermeer (*vur*-MARE). If the Baroque outside of Holland can be compared to heroic poetry, then the Golden Age of Dutch Painting—the seventeenth century—except for the achievement of the giants Hals and, above all, Rembrandt, can be identified as smooth, perfect prose.

How is it possible to paint so that the color seems literally breathed onto the canvas? How is a ruff painted so starchily stiff, yet with such evident elasticity? How is the translucency of the headband achieved, or the reflected color in the cheek? What of the hands, drawn in color, plump but resilient? And the edges of dress and ruff, swimming in light and air? And see what subtle calculations are found in the angle of the ruff, the off-vertical of the gold brocade, and the petal-like expansion of the handkerchief and the lace at the wrists! Cover the salmon-pink bag and see how much is lost. In this painting by Hals, the earliest great master of the Dutch Golden Age, the sitter hardly exists except as an element of a picture and a miracle of pure painting. Hals lived in careless poverty and died in the poorhouse. He was a virtuoso of slashing brushwork, but his soberest portraits have worn best. Like Philippe de Champaigne, he usually observed without comment, but he dealt with a different level of society—the solid citizenry. Most good paintings, it is said, foster the desire to paint, but some great paintings produce only the thought of laying brushes aside in despair. And so it is here.

21. *Portrait of a Lady in a Ruff*

by HALS (Dutch, c. 1580-1666)

J. H. Wade Collection

A coin symbolic of eighteenth-century France would bear the legend "Age of Reason" on one side and a scene of the joy of life on the other, in a style of sinuous curves and shell-like grace called "Rococo." Our Puritan background often makes it difficult to succumb to this frivolous, carefree art; yet what pleasure it affords! Rubens' lusty nymphs and satyrs recede and his color is transformed into pastel hues depicting playful lords and ladies of the court. Watteau (*vaht*-TOE) was the first master of the century, with his nervous but sure drawing and gentle art. His architectural setting is more playful and less grandiose than those of the seventeenth century—an intimate stage with a scenic backdrop. In this never-never land the delicately formed figures pirouette, play, and make love without regard to the onlooker, of whom they are either unaware or disdainful. All of the large, sweeping movements of the Baroque are reduced to small, curling ones, as in the shimmer of the drapery, or the rhythmic, fluffy foliage. This *Dancing Party* once belonged to Frederick the Great (1712-1786) and remained at Potsdam in the collection of the German emperors until 1918.

At the other end of Gallery Eight hangs *Citizen Crouzet* (*kroo*-ZAY), painted by Jacques Louis David (*dah*-VEED) about 1795. Not "Lady This" or "Countess That," but "Citizen"! The very title tells us something of the changes wrought by the French Revolution. Artists were encouraged by the State to paint severely, morally, democratically, and to use subjects from republican Rome—Jupiter and Mars gave way to Brutus and Horatio. David, a pupil of Boucher, a great artist of the old regime, lived to sketch Marie Antoinette on the way to the guillotine and to become painter to Napoleon. This portrait is idealized, in the spirit of Classical models, although the head is individualized. The pose is particularly original and stresses the long arcs of arm and dress. The artist created an even play of light that steals around such forms as the back of the neck and the half-hidden right arm. In keeping with the new austerity, color was subdued and made secondary to modeling. This sculptural ideal, which recalls Florentine Renaissance painting, dominated the Neo-Classic and Academic schools of the early nineteenth century.

22. *Dancing Party in a Pavilion*

by WATTEAU (French, 1684-1721)

Louis D. Beaumont Collection

23. *Citizen Crouzet*

by JACQUES LOUIS DAVID

(French, 1748-1825)

Grace Rainey Rogers Collection

Turner is the great English artist of the Romantic Period, a Lord Byron of paint and color. No aspect of nature was too vast or cataclysmic for his canvases: *The Falls of the Rhine; The Slave Ship; Snowstorm; The Burning of the Houses of Parliament*. Restraint, intellect, drawing, and clarity were thrown overboard for freedom, imagination, color, and mystery. In this picture the swarming multitudes of London ebb and flow at the edges of the canvas, overwhelmed by a vast force of nature, the raging fire reflected in the wide, impassive Thames. Turner went much further than the Venetians in his obsession with color and light. One might say he was an Impressionist before Impressionism. Hardly a shape has a sharp contour, and yet the whole composition has the impact of reality on a heroic scale. Turner witnessed the historic destruction of the Houses of Parliament, but painted the picture from memory. His hastiness is more apparent than real. The discipline and calculation behind the romantic fervor give this masterpiece its depth and richness.

24. Burning of the Houses of Parliament

by TURNER (English, 1775-1851)

John L. Severance Collection

25. Antibes

by MONET (French, 1840-1926)

J. H. Wade Collection

SLIDE 25

In its light, clear color, this picture in Gallery Nine is different from all the others that we have seen. No matter how rich the hues, how convincing the light, the Old Masters have in common a "studio" vision—an almost twilight appearance. In the 1870s a group of painters, derisively dubbed "Impressionists," adopted a totally new approach to light. They knew that light and color were indivisible, that light was color and color suggested light, and that this vision was best obtained out-of-doors. By using small strokes of varied hues, they approached the brilliant, shifting effect of sunlight. Monet's (*moh*-NAY's) picture of Antibes on the Mediterranean is a masterpiece of Impressionism, a fresh and poetic examination of the pearly, hazy, hot, and evanescent sunlight of the Riviera. Monet's dominant interest was neither Poussin's ordered, nor Turner's romantic, landscape, but the landscape of the city vacationer who looks at the landscape without being a part of it. In this limited sense, Impressionist paintings are abstract landscapes, the true subject being light. Form dissolved completely as the aged Monet's last canvases recorded more and more transient effects—the traces momentarily left by light as it changed. Monet seemed a relic of the nineteenth century when he died in 1926, but his last works inspire much of our current abstract art.

26. Race Horses

by DEGAS (French, 1834-1917) *Bequest of Leonard C. Hanna, Jr.*

Across the gallery is this brilliant pastel by Degas (*deh*-GAH), showing a different side of Impressionism. The artist was a master draftsman and, unlike Monet, painted few landscapes. The broken color gives a luminous effect and the pastel hues are unusually well preserved for this fragile chalk medium. The startling composition, heavily weighted to the left, with the horse at the far left arbitrarily cut off, is a cue to the dominant theme of the picture—a casual spontaneity. It owes much to photography, with its quality of momentarily arrested movement. Degas was an avid student of photographs and was one of the first creative artists to find inspiration from this new art form. The seemingly haphazard arrangement has a purposefully erratic rhythm, like horses milling before the start. It is held in place by the three sturdy, evenly spaced trees, and by the unified texture and color of the grass. The artist's classical discipline in drawing is shown to great advantage in the sure depiction of the horses. A crusty bachelor conscious of his aristocratic background, Degas often treated his subjects—chiefly women and horses—with a lack of respect that borders on contempt.

Degas' horses were observed objectively, even coldly—an attitude impossible to the warm-hearted Renoir (*renn*-WAHR). Like Rubens, whom he admired, Renoir celebrated the joy of life—of the bourgeois, not the aristocratic, world. His paintings are proof that great art is not necessarily tragic. Even when sick and old, Renoir had a paintbrush strapped to his stiffened arthritic hand—and his last canvases were as joyous as his first. However, mere optimism is not enough, and Renoir's works stand or fall on their complex harmonies of light and color, with their flowing composition, sure placement of figures in space, and undulating rhythm. The dancing rhythms of *The Apple Seller* are due as much to the brushwork as to the dappled sunlight. Whereas some Impressionists painted in small, short brush strokes, Renoir could not resist using his brush in something like the fluid and sensuous eighteenth-century manner. Harmonies can be traced throughout this painting: note that the salmon pink of the little girl's costume is placed against a white dress with a supporting touch of pink, and that the blue fabrics nearby have pink highlights. Paintings like this, beloved today, were hooted at by visitors to the early Impressionist exhibitions.

27. *The Apple Seller*

by RENOIR (French, 1841-1919)

Bequest of Leonard C. Hanna, Jr.

If Renoir commented joyously on life, then Toulouse-Lautrec (*too*-LOOZE *loh*-TREK) was his opposite, for his comments were usually acid. Crippled and stunted at an early age by a fall from a horse, Toulouse-Lautrec, an aristocrat by birth, chose to live in the dissipation and squalor of Montmartre's low life. His subject matter was drawn from the night life of Paris: M. Boileau (*bwah*-LOW) was a semigenteel bouncer for a Parisian scandal sheet, and his blue jowls, broad torso, and self-satisfied air seem most appropriate to his position. Lautrec delights in such tidbits as the stiff-necked, square-headed man to the right, or the incongruous combination of stovepipe hat and fur-collared coat of his tablemate. The deliberately tilted perspective of the table top is necessary as a foil for the expansive M. Boileau. The vibrating, artificial illumination of the café is a unifying factor, as is the hasty but incisive brushwork. The milky-green of the liquid in the tumbler—undoubtedly absinthe—is a sinister accent as essential to this picture as the pink purse is to the portrait by Hals. But the color, intensifying the mood of the picture, seems a fitting projection of the deformed artist's satiric interests, which were fittingly expressed with a linear mastery not unlike that of Degas.

28. *Monsieur Boileau in a Café*

by TOULOUSE-LAUTREC

(French, 1864-1901)

Hinman B. Hurlbut Collection

29. *Pigeon Tower at Montbriand*

by CEZANNE (French, 1839-1906)   *The James W. Corrigan Memorial*

While the bright color and outdoor atmosphere of *The Pigeon Tower* speak of its Impressionist origins, the obviously solid and carefully organized composition is a significant departure for its time. Cézanne is the leading figure of the Post-Impressionists, who include such notables as the later Renoir, Gauguin (*goh*-GANN), and Van Gogh (*van* GOH). They came "after Impressionism" and went beyond it. Cézanne combined Impressionist technical innovations with a more solid structure. *The Pigeon Tower* stresses firmly interwoven horizontals and verticals formed by systematic brush textures and color variations in foliage. The loosely painted, vibrating net of the sky is opposed by the solid orange-tan ground. The spaces in the grove are clearly established, especially the circular opening around the tower. The aim of the artist was expressed in his famous statement that he wished to "revive Poussin in the contact with nature"—that is, to adapt Poussin's solid structure to Nature's loose forms. His remarks on the *construction* of basic forms, to "see in nature the cylinder, the sphere, the cone . . . " have been interpreted as prophetic of the Cubist and abstract movements. In one sense this is so, for Cézanne was above all not interested in subject matter but in pictures as the realization of sensations.

30. The Call

by GAUGUIN (French, 1848-1903)

Gift of Hanna Fund and

Leonard C. Hanna, Jr.

Unlike Cézanne, Gauguin found subject matter to be of absorbing interest. This city-bred ex-stockbroker traveled restlessly to the West Indies, to Tahiti, to the Marquesas, in search of meaningful images that he could not find in civilized Europe. His uneasy quest of the romantic, the exotic, and the primitive resulted in monumental canvases, often of enigmatic subjects, painted with muted but sensuous colors in flat patterns. The title describes the action of the figure to the right; but whom does she call? And what of the mysterious gaze of the central figure? Gauguin, like medieval artists, seems to speak in symbols, but his meanings are personal—they do not belong to society at large—and hence their vagueness and mystery, which prefigure Surrealism. The artist partially succeeded in discarding many layers of civilized convention to arrive at an imagined ideal—basic man, primitive and free. But works like this Marquesas picture of 1902 are equally important for the decorative power of the flowers and rocks of the foreground or the almost Japanese subtlety to be seen in the calculated arrangement of the trees. The colors are not modeled and, like those of cloisonné enamel, are separated only by contour lines.

Van Gogh and Gauguin worked side by side in Arles, but their personalities were as incompatible as their art. Both were interested in subject matter, but for the Dutch-born Van Gogh the subject was not a romantic flight from reality but a means of passionate, humanitarian, and personal involvement. *Mlle. Ravoux* (*rah*-VOO) was done in 1890, the year of Van Gogh's suicide, and yet the reference to it in his letter to his brother Theo is matter-of-fact: "Last week I did a portrait of a girl of 16 or nearly, in blue against a blue background, the daughter of the people where I am staying. I have given her this portrait, but I made a variation of it for you." The haunting anxiety of the eyes and the tension between the acid blue of the background and the lemon yellows of the face are echoed by the vibrant, staccato brushwork. The painfully personal and poignant self-revelation recalls the mood of the late Rembrandt, and the distortions in the head are in the expressive tradition of El Greco and Grünewald (GRIH-*neh-vahlt*). Van Gogh's artistic salvation was in the local, the particular. In the artist's words, the wise man does not spend his time in science or politics, but "studies a single blade of grass."

31. *Mademoiselle Ravoux*

by VAN GOGH (Dutch, 1853-1890)   *Bequest of Leonard C. Hanna, Jr.*

32. *La Vie*

by PICASSO (Spanish, born 1881)

Gift of Hanna Fund

The sixty years of Picasso's (*pee*-KAH-*so's*) art cover the modern era. No other artist has ever been so prominent for so long—or so deservedly—for he still paints with an inventiveness and power that would be astounding in a young man. Playful, individual, appealing or repellent, suave or brutal, his great talent is as easy and fertile as that of Rubens. A Spaniard by birth, he is recognized as the leading painter of France and of the world. Of all his styles, from close representation to the almost abstract, the Blue Period of 1902-5 and the Rose Period of 1905-6 are the most popular, for they appeal directly to our emotions. During the Blue Period, Picasso elongated his figures in an effort to arouse our sympathy for the miserable persons depicted in gloomy blue. One can only speculate about the meaning of this large picture, for, like Gauguin, Picasso uses personal symbolism, which can mean many things. The nude couple seem united in their distance from the heavily draped mother and child. Do the latter represent conventional stability against which youth and art revolt? Are the huddled figures on the stone reliefs turning inward upon themselves in order to escape from an alien, intolerable world? Or, is the picture as a whole, with its several different styles, an allegory of birth, youth, and age—the stages of man?

People who live in Cleveland and nearby know how many different attractions the Museum offers in addition to its major function of preserving and displaying the art of the ages. In all seasons there are activities such as lectures, motion picture programs, classes for all ages in the practice and appreciation of art, musical concerts, and tours of the Museum. Most of these activities are free, and I want to invite you to attend them whenever you visit our city. If you live in this area, you are encouraged to make regular use of the cultural opportunities which our staff provides. Our Museum becomes richer in great art as the days go by, and these treasures are gathered and preserved here for your enjoyment and edification. You are always welcome.

Sherman E. Lee